the One Wind

Gill Davies

The One Wind

First published 2008

© SeaSquirt Books 2008

Ty Ganol Rhodiad y Brenin St Davids Pembrokeshire Wales

ISBN 978-1-905470-22-8

British Library CIP Data

A catalogue record of this book is available from the British Library

Series concept David Hughes

Written by Gill Davies

Printed and bound by Gomer Press Limited, Wales

Contents

About the paper on which *The One Wind* is printed

Paper is made from fibres that are found in the cell walls of all plants. The fibres mainly come from plant sources such as wood, bamboo, cotton, jute, or even rice. However, wood from trees is the main source of fibres used in paper making. A mixture of water and fibres is filtered through a screen to make a sheet of paper. When the paper is dried chemical bonds form to give the paper its strength.

The One Wind is printed on paper in which at least 75% of the fibre has been recycled. This means it comes from materials that have been used before.

The main sources from which recycled paper is made are newspapers, magazines, directories, leaflets, office and computer paper, cardboard from boxes and packing, mixed or coloured papers.

NAPM approved
recycled product

This book is printed on Revive Matt from the Robert Horne Group. It contains at least 75% de-inked post-consumer waste fibre.

The One Wind

As the One Wind blows . . .
a message is delivered all around the globe.

Helped by two special friends – the first one an eagle,
a bird of the land and the second one an albatross, a
bird of the sea – the One Wind takes a vital message
to all the world, and in particular to mankind. He warns
of the damage that is being done in all the different
habitats and the desperately urgent need to deal with
this ever-growing problem.

As the verses flow, buffeted along by the spirit of
the One Wind over field and woodland, ocean and snow,
jungle and grassland, mountain, desert and finally to
cities where people cower from his ferocious force,
we share the magic of each very special environment.
Helped by the birds, the One Wind's urgent message
is clear. We must save these wonderful wild places
and all the amazing creatures that live there.

Gill Davies

7

The One Wind blew!

The One Wind blew!
And wildly as the One Wind blew . . .
the meadow grasses bent and swirled
soft petals scattered, blossoms whirled
small mice scampered, whiskers twirled
a scarecrow's scarf unravelled, unfurled
to flutter like the crows, feather-tossed and curled.

Then, as the One Wind wilder blew . . .
it gained in strength, it rose, it suddenly grew . . .
the forest shuddered as it hurtled through;
as the squirrels hid, owls woke and flew
in skies swept startling clean bright blue,
as the dry leaves rattled and danced anew,
scitter-scatter-scutter as the One Wind blew.

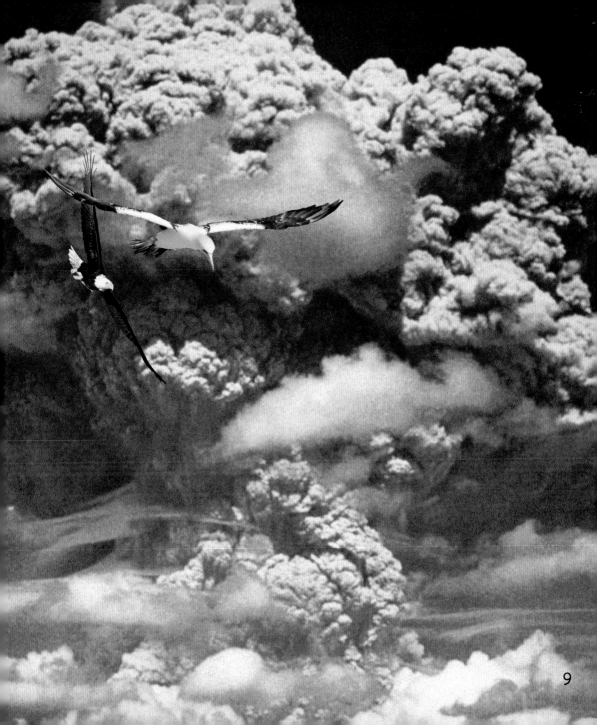

Two brave birds

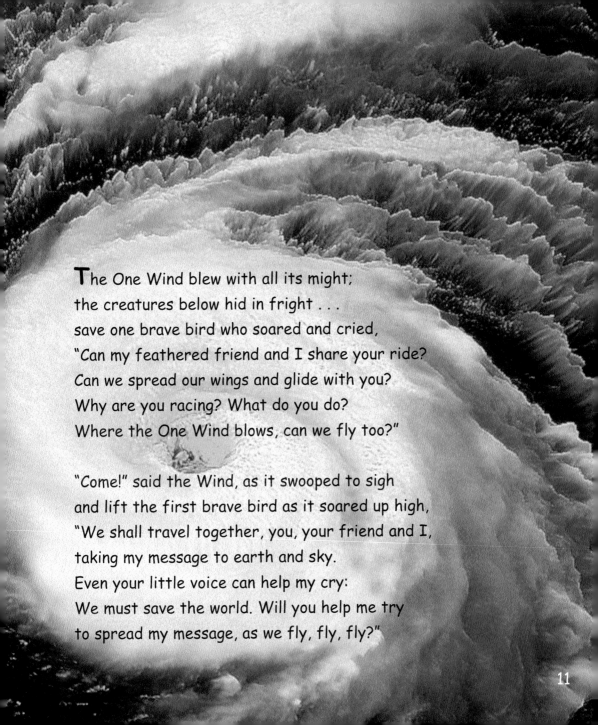

The One Wind blew with all its might;
the creatures below hid in fright . . .
save one brave bird who soared and cried,
"Can my feathered friend and I share your ride?
Can we spread our wings and glide with you?
Why are you racing? What do you do?
Where the One Wind blows, can we fly too?"

"Come!" said the Wind, as it swooped to sigh
and lift the first brave bird as it soared up high,
"We shall travel together, you, your friend and I,
taking my message to earth and sky.
Even your little voice can help my cry:
We must save the world. Will you help me try
to spread my message, as we fly, fly, fly?"

A sunset lake

The One Wind soared as the first bird skimmed
where a sunset glowed and a lake was rimmed
with twilight rose and a frieze of trees
that swayed to the evening's gentle breeze.
"We must tell all the creatures and spirits of earth
they must fight to survive from the moment of birth
and remind mankind what the world is worth."

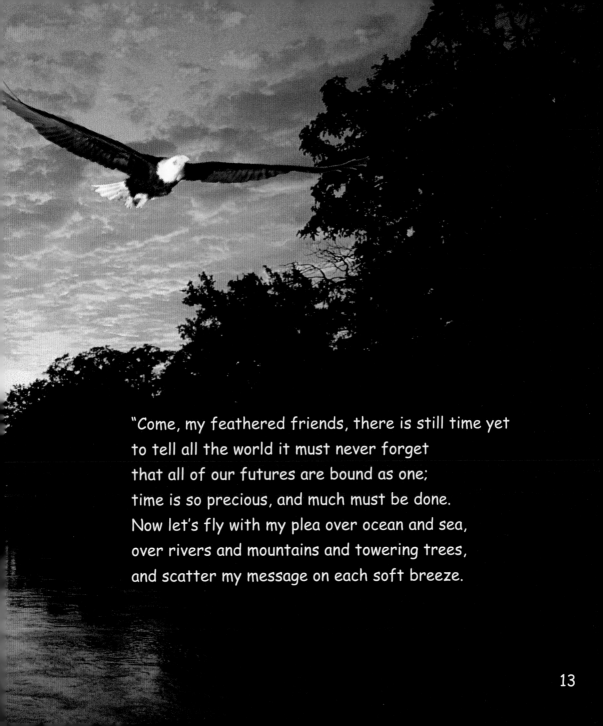

"Come, my feathered friends, there is still time yet
to tell all the world it must never forget
that all of our futures are bound as one;
time is so precious, and much must be done.
Now let's fly with my plea over ocean and sea,
over rivers and mountains and towering trees,
and scatter my message on each soft breeze.

13

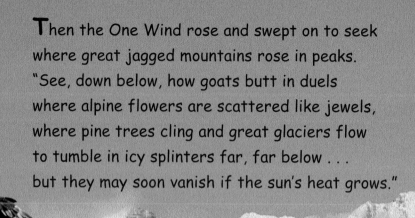

Then the One Wind rose and swept on to seek
where great jagged mountains rose in peaks.
"See, down below, how goats butt in duels
where alpine flowers are scattered like jewels,
where pine trees cling and great glaciers flow
to tumble in icy splinters far, far below . . .
but they may soon vanish if the sun's heat grows."

Mountain and meadow

Rivers need this water; watch how they flow,
surging in the summer with the melting snow,
taking moisture to land and field as they go,
between reeds and meadows where wild flowers grow.
While birds sing above and fish frolic below,
and in limpid pools, frog snouts show
while herons stand tall on one tiptoe.

Next the Wind sailed south to where lions lazed
in the African plains as great elephants grazed,
where giraffes walked on stilts above warthogs plump
and black stripes dazzled on the zebra's rump . . .
The Wind cried, "Each creature needs its own space;
Each to its own and each in its place,
but land for the farmers is spreading apace."

Plains

"People need food and so fields expand
but the animals too have a right to their land.
Cruel poachers kill elephant and rhino too,
whatever the wardens try bravely to do."
The One Wind breathed a heavy heartfelt sigh
and blew on the herds that were passing by:
"May your lives be long and I hope you thrive."

Then the One Wind blew where thick jungles grew
as the hot air shimmered and bright parrots flew.
"Men are chopping down trees, and too soon, too fast,
rainforests will vanish and be part of our past.
This rich steamy splendour must be saved to stay,
not turned into dust that the storms blow away,
sweeping emerald bright into dull barren grey.

These vital trees make rich oxygen:
The world will change if this resource is gone:
Lost will be tigers and orchids and soldier ants
the leopard that leaps, then rests and pants,
huge butterflies, snapping crocodiles,
orangutans with sad winsome smiles,
and snakes coiled in slithering, glittering piles.

Jungles

Sea

The One Wind now surged over ocean and sea
where gaint whales spouted, joyous and free:
The Wind roared, "Splendid, creatures, let's race, let's fly!"
He blew mountainous waves that rose sky high;
and the whales sped forward for all they were worth,
encircling the orb of the great globe's girth
as the dolphins grinned, blowing bubbles of mirth.

Then the albatross soared, slicing the air,
crying, "Save this please; Oh, mercy! Does anyone care?"
to the squid and the octopus, their tentacles flowing;
past coral-reef creatures and jellyfish glowing,
past fishes like worms, and many with fins,
past the fearsome sharks with sharp-toothed grins,
past crabs, eels, and catfish with whiskery chins.

Soon the One Wind was blowing much drier air:
There was sand in his bellows, sand in his hair,
as he showed the eagle the desert and dune,
glowing golden and red in the white heat of noon.
"You think nothing moves but that's a mistake;
vultures fly high above those zig-zagging snakes.
Lizards bask; camels gasp as the hot sun bakes."

Desert

"See, the cactus casts shadows, it will soon be night;
the desert cools fast in the bright moonlight.
Many creatures emerge both to hunt and eat
and the sand is busy-busy with scurrying feet."
The first bird stared as a scorpion appeared
with a threatening sting raised up sharp at its rear
near a fennec fox with enormous ears.

The One Wind now flew from one pole to the other
to see what his bird of the seas might discover:
Here was snow, here was ice, freezing cold everywhere;
One Wind's breath turned to frost and it hung in the air,
as he shouted, "Look! Over there! Over there!
A polar bear is standing and sniffing the air
but if the ice caps should melt, he will disappear."

Ice and snow

The foxes and hares were snow white here;
there were great tusked walruses, seals, reindeer.
Down south waddled penguins, off for a slide
or to hitch a lift on a glacier ride.
The Wind caressed icebergs, gleaming like glass.
"If the ice caps vanish, all this will pass –
for this glorious playground is melting fast."

Village and city

Thus the One Wind swept all around the world,
and, as each busy nation below them unfurled,
he urged all the creatures to try to survive;
then begged all the people, "Help them stay alive."
He gusted through the villages, swept through the towns,
till the streets of the cities filled with howling sounds,
Shaking the buildings, till the people crouched down.

"Ahoy!" cried the Wind, in a furious rage,
"Act fast, take control; it's a critical stage.
The world needs your help, and I need you too:
Mend your ways, think ahead, plan what to do.
You must add your strength to my One Wind powers.
Don't squander resources, don't waste precious hours.
The ice caps are drowning this one world of ours."

Now the two birds longed for their soft warm nests
as the One Wind sighed into whispering rest
and drew a shuddering breath, then yawned, "It is done!
We have taken my message to everyone
while you've warmed my heart with your companionship,
and softened the edges of my temper's whip."
Into deep slumber soon the One Wind would slip.

Beautiful Earth

And as The One Wind subsided and sank down to rest
both the birds promised, "We shall do our best
to tell all the creatures that fly in the air
to help carry the message; so please don't despair.
If we all spread the word and we truly do care
the world will survive for us all to share.
. . . this beautiful Earth, this planet so rare."

End and beginning

All the world's birds watched . . .

Every bird watched and waited as the two birds flew
down to rest at last, past the glistening dew.
Down to special safe perches, on soft drifting wings,
too weary to think, as the dawn birds sing.
The journey was done, this first task was complete . . .
Now it was time for rest and sleep so sweet
and dreams of a world with just one heartbeat.

The One Wind blew!

In his swirling sleep, the One Wind blew:
In shifting dreams he blew, blew, blew,
making the world good and new
to itself and its creatures
one heart true . . .

The One Wind blew.

the One

Series of eco-aware books

This book was designed and typeset by
Playne Books Limited
Park Court Barn
Trefin
Haverfordwest
Pembrokeshire
SA62 5AU

All the photographs are from Playne Books photographic library.